Self
DISCIPLINE
SOLUTION

*Build habits
to reach goals
faster*

MIKE EIMAN

To Alexis,
Who pushed me to pursue my goals.

Self Discipline Solution: Build Habits to Reach Goals Faster

Copyright © 2017 Mike Eiman

All Rights Reserved.

No part of this book may be reproduced in any form or by any means without permission in writing from the publisher, except for the inclusion of brief quotations in a review.

Visit the author's website at www.mikeeiman.com.

Although the author and publisher have made every effort to ensure that the information in this book was correct at press time, the author and publisher do not assume and hereby disclaim any liability to any party for any loss, damage, or disruption caused by errors or omissions, whether such errors or omissions result from negligence, accident, or any other cause.

ISBN: 9781549756573

Contents

Introduction: Don't Make Your Bed   1

Chapter 1: The Goldfish Myth   11
    Taught to Believe   14
    Change Your Story   16
    Swim Against the Stream   18

Chapter 2: The Story of Self Discipline   21
    Elimination   24
    Detox   26
    Replacement   27
    Next Steps   28

Chapter 3: Goals & Priorities   **29**
  What You Do (and Don't)   32
  Two Hours to Dream   35
  A Worthy Sacrifice   36

Chapter 4: Avoid Backsliding   **39**
  The Fast Track to Failure   43
  Easy Pieces   44
  Keep Yourself Accountable   46

Chapter 5: Become a Constant Learner   **49**
  Try New Habits   53
  Learn New Skills   54
  Change Your Strategy   55
  A Final Caution   56

Chapter 6: Make Mistakes Every Day   **59**
  Know Thy Self   62
  Learn From Failure   64
  When to Quit   65

Chapter 7: Dealing With Burnout   **67**
  Climbing Mt. Everest   71
  Setting Small Goals   72

Take a Break	73
Talk About It	75
Chapter 8: Be An Inspiration	**77**
Never Imitate	81
Summary: A Quick Review	**85**
About the Author	**96**

A Foolish Consistency

"A foolish consistency is the hobgoblin of little minds, adored by little statesmen and philosophers and divines. With consistency a great soul has simply nothing to do. He may as well concern himself with his shadow on the wall. Speak what you think now in hard words, and to-morrow speak what to-morrow thinks in hard words again, though it contradict every thing you said to-day. — 'Ah, so you shall be sure to be misunderstood.' — Is it so bad, then, to be misunderstood? Pythagoras was misunderstood, and Socrates, and Jesus, and Luther, and Copernicus, and Galileo, and Newton, and every pure and wise spirit that ever took flesh. To be great is to be misunderstood."

From Self Reliance
by Ralph Waldo Emerson

Introduction
Don't Make Your Bed

*"As you make your bed,
so you must lie upon it."*
— Proverb

Whether you're tackling a creative project, sticking with a new diet or adopting a daily exercise regime, you need extraordinary self-discipline. Fortunately, most people have so little self-discipline that you can become extraordinary with far less effort that you might expect.

Self-discipline is about doing what most people won't do. You can't become exceptional by imitating ordinary people.

So many books and articles claim that self-discipline starts with something simple like making your bed every morning. Maybe you've tried it. The theory is that by starting each day with a small victory, you're setting the stage to accomplish more during the day.

Hogwash.

The only benefit you're likely to gain from this exercise is that you'll get really good at making your bed. It will make you really disciplined in one area without helping you improve yourself in areas that actually count.

Any ideas you have about self-discipline are mostly wrong. You probably think "self-discipline" means having a life that runs like clockwork, where every minute of your day is meticulously plotted on a calendar.

These flawed ideas come from books, podcasts and videos about business, entrepreneurship and personal development. Self-discipline is a state of mind, not a collection of worksheets and exercises. You already have perfect self-discipline, just not in the areas of your life where it actually matters to you.

Don't Make Your Bed

For instance, you might be quite disciplined about watching Netflix for three hours every night before bed. Or watching football every Sunday. Or eating meals at the same times every day. But when it comes to developing your new business idea, working on a creative project or even catching up on housework — you're a complete train wreck.

Popular self-help gurus and click-bait articles on the web give lots of bad advice to help you develop self-discipline. They tell you to do things like:

- Go to bed earlier and wake up earlier.
- Set a time each day to focus on your project.
- Visualize yourself completing the project before you start.
- Make a list of your goals
- Meditate
- Be persistent

You've probably tried one or more of these methods. Maybe some of them worked, or maybe they didn't. Such advice may not be deliberately bad, but it fails to consider why you aren't already doing the things you want to be doing.

Let's say you want to get your finances in order. If all you had to do was learn how to focus on the problem, you'd be a millionaire by now. If meditation could make you wealthy, the Dalai Lama would be richer than Bill Gates. People focus on their problems 24 hours a day. They think about their problems all day long, and let those problems marinate while they sleep.

Very few people lack the self-discipline to focus on a problem. Where most of us go wrong is in how we think about the problem. When you start thinking about why you want to exercise or start a new diet, you might say something like:

- I want to be thinner.
- I want to have more energy.
- I want to live longer.

These are all good reasons to exercise and eat better. They're sensible, logical reasons to take action. But none of these reasons will inspire you to change your habits or develop serious self-discipline. That kind of inspiration comes from a good story, not a good reason.

What's the difference between a story and a reason?

A reason is a logical explanation you have to justify a personal or professional goal. Wanting to pay your bills on time is a good reason to improve your finances, but it lacks any emotional weight. Someone with a good reason will start strong and fizzle out when things get too difficult.

If you want to take lasting action, you need a good story behind your reason. For example:

If I don't eat better and exercise, I'm going to have a heart attack just like my father did.

I need to take better care of myself so I don't become a burden on my children when I'm older.

No matter how much I sleep, I'm always tired. If I don't do something soon, I'm probably going to get in a car accident / walk into oncoming traffic.

These stories put something at stake. There are physical and emotional consequences for failure to make progress.

We'll go into more detail about the power of stories later in this book. Right now, you need to think about whether your life is driven by logical reasons or inspirational stories. This is what separates those with strong self-discipline from those who spend their lives jumping haphazardly from one project to another.

This is the part where most self-help books would tell you to get a sheet of paper and write down all the logical reasons you have for your goals so that we can convert them into stories in later chapter. I'm not going to tell you to do that.

Why?

Because you already know what your biggest goal or problem is. You know what your logical reasons are for pursuing that goal. And you know that a lack of self-discipline has prevented you from reaching that goal. For some reason, you can't force yourself to put in the daily effort required to achieve your dreams.

You won't learn self-discipline by doing things that are comfortable or familiar. If you're reading this, you've read other books and articles on the subject that have left you feeling more confused than when you started. This is perfectly normal. But at some point, you have to stop looking for different versions of the same information that didn't work the first time you tried it. You need a new approach.

You need *The Self Discipline Solution*.

The Self Discipline Solution

In the following chapters, we'll analyze the thoughts behind your lack of discipline and start transforming your old, worn-out reasons into new and exciting stories. Feel free to write things down as you go. Sometimes writing out your thoughts helps to cement the ideas better in your mind.

But more than likely, the best ideas will come to you when you least expect it.

Chapter 1
The Goldfish Myth

*"Whether you think you can,
or you think you can't--you're right."*
— *Henry Ford*

We've all heard about goldfish having really short attention spans. The myth says that a goldfish can live happily in a small bowl because it can only pay attention for a few seconds. It swims a lap around the bowl, forgets where it was a few seconds earlier and repeats the process.

Goldfish are actually smarter than this. Some scientific studies have suggested that goldfish can learn to operate a food dispenser that only works at a set time each day. One study found that goldfish actually retained this skill after being released into the wild and recaptured five months later.

Taught to Believe

Despite being totally wrong, we hear the Goldfish Myth repeated constantly as if it's true. We believe the story — hook, line and sinker.

There's a good chance you're in the same boat. You tell yourself over and over again (or your friends and family tell you) that you lack the self-discipline to achieve your goals. As a result, you start to believe the story even if the evidence doesn't support it. That's not to say that you'd be more disciplined if only you *believed* in yourself. People believe all kinds of ridiculous things about themselves that are obviously wrong.

Consider a 6-year-old girl who loves to sing along with her favorite songs. She can't carry a tune, but she loves the feeling of singing. One day her mother, unable to tolerate another mi-

The Goldfish Myth

nute of dissonant shrieking, tells the girl that she's a terrible singer and she should stop trying.

The girl is saddened by her mother's words, but doesn't allow that to deter her love of music. The next day, the girl auditions for the school choir. The choir director hears the girl sing and tells her she'll never be a singer.

"Study hard and do your homework," the director says. "But choir isn't for you."

By the time a few more people tell the girl how bad her singing is, she calls it quits.

If you haven't succeeded in becoming more disciplined, it's likely because you have a Goldfish Myth of your own. Here are some examples of myths you might have told yourself:

"I can't manage my finances because I'm terrible at math.

"I'll never be able to complete this project. I can't focus."

"How can I start my own business? Business is too complicated."

"I've always wanted to learn how to play guitar (or some other musical instrument), but my hands are too big/small/uncoordinated."

These are all stories you may have told yourself at one point or another. Maybe you've even overcome some of them. The key to overcoming these stories is to start recognizing them.

Change Your Story

It's really that simple. Whenever you catch yourself reciting some ancient myth about why you can't do something, make a mental note. You might have a genuine handicap that will keep you from your goal. For instance, if you're 5 feet tall, nearsighted and have flat feet, you're unlikely to qualify as a Navy fighter pilot or play basketball in the NBA.

But when you decide something is impossible because you're "bad at math" or "not talented

The Goldfish Myth

enough," there's a good chance you're caught a self-fulfilling prophesy.

Any task can be made impossible by believing it's impossible. Why? Because when you believe a thing is impossible, you're less likely to take action. And if you do take action, you probably won't give it your best effort. Imagine if your parents had told you as a child that it was impossible to tie your shoes; that you would never be intelligent or coordinated enough to do it yourself. You would be conditioned to believe this story until someone else showed you otherwise.

The reverse is not always true. You can't necessarily achieve the impossible through belief alone. Believing you can fly will not allow you to sprout wings if you jump off a skyscraper. However, the belief that men could fly did lead to the invention of the airplane.

Self-discipline starts with identifying the stories you tell yourself. Which stories are helping you? Which ones are hurting you?

Then you just need to change the stories that are holding you back from your full potential. It's a simple concept that takes some serious effort to implement. Hey, if it were easy you would have done it by now. The following chapters will walk you through the process.

Swim Against the Stream

One more thing before moving on to the nuts and bolts of *The Self Discipline Solution*. A lot of the things in this book will require you to do things that your peers don't do, or won't do. That means you must be prepared for others to mock and ridicule you.

Ordinary people don't understand why anyone would try to be different. After all, being ordinary works just fine for most people. They go to school, get a job, make as much money as their boss is willing to pay them, start a family, buy a house, retire, and work on their hobbies until they die.

The Goldfish Myth

That life is fine. There's nothing wrong with it. Unless it's not the life you want for yourself. If you're reading a book like this, you probably want an uncommonly fine life. Then you have to be the goldfish that swims the other way.

Against the stream.

Chapter 2
The Story of Self Discipline

It's easier to prevent bad habits than to break them.
— Benjamin Franklin

What is the first thing you do upon waking every morning? Maybe you brush your teeth, make a pot of coffee, eat breakfast or take a shower. Or maybe you throw on some clothes, choke down a breakfast bar and dash off to work.

Now think about the last thing you typically do before bed each night. You might change your clothes, do some reading, watch a little TV, eat a late-night snack or any number of other tasks.

Whatever your routines are, you have developed a level of discipline to be able to repeat that pattern on a daily basis. Even if your routines are counterproductive, they require so much self-discipline that it becomes second nature.

Most people think the first step to becoming more disciplined is to add tasks to their existing routines. Unfortunately, they've got it all backwards. Self-discipline starts with elimination.

Elimination

No matter what anyone tells you, it's easier to <u>not</u> do something than it is to <u>do</u> something. How much time or effort does it take to not work on achieving your goals? Exactly zero.

If you're always rushing in the morning because you're late for work, consider what you can stop doing before you start adding things to your plate. Maybe you like to stay up until midnight watching Netflix or playing video games. When your alarm goes off in the morning, you're too tired to do anything but push the snooze button.

The Story of Self Discipline

At this point, you're probably saying something like, "I see where this is going. I'll just turn off the TV an hour earlier. Problem solved." But you can't be trusted. You've developed **Extreme Discipline**, which runs so deep in your subconscious that it becomes a part of your identity. Extreme Discipline is like an addiction. Simply cutting back on these habits is bound to fail.

Sure, you may be able to turn off the TV and go to bed earlier for a few days, weeks or months. But you will almost certainly slip back into your old ways. It's like a former smoker who lights up a cigarette to cope with a stressful situation. Before long, they're puffing away like they never quit in the first place.

Instead of convincing yourself to "cut back a little," you need to stop these Extreme Disciplines entirely.

Detox

You might assume the next step after Elimination is to replace your old habit with something else. Wrong.

If you give up a habit for which you've developed Extreme Discipline, your brain will have a hissy fit. Trying to add new habits or routines too soon will only make things worse.

Studies have shown it takes about 30 days to form a new habit. That means it could take a month to simply adjust to quitting an old habit. If you try to add in new routines too soon, you're likely to revert back to your old ways quicker. Remember, it's easier not to do something than it is to do something.

The Detox period should last at least seven days. You'll know you're still detoxing as long as you get a strong urge to continue your old habit. For instance, continuing the Netflix example, you may be tempted to watch an episode of your favorite TV show.

The Story of Self Discipline

"Come on," you say. "It's just one episode. I'll be in bed by 10 o'clock. What's the big deal?"

That's the sound of failure. As long as you're coming up with excuses for why it's OK to give in to your addiction, you're not ready to move on.

Replacement

You may have already figured this out, but it's almost impossible to get through the Detox phase without doing something to replace the old habit. If you're trying to win back some free time by eliminating four hours of daily TV watching, you've got four extra hours to fill.

So you're probably already making better use of your time. But it doesn't mean anything until you're fully detoxed. Good for you if you've managed to replace a bad habit with a good one for a few days. Unfortunately, the replacement phase doesn't start until you've detoxed for at least seven days, preferably 30 days).

Next Steps

How do you know what to eliminate? What should you replace your bad habits with? It all depends on your goals, which is exactly what we'll cover in the next chapter.

Chapter 3
Goals & Priorities

"Action expresses priorities."
— Mahatma Gandhi

Deciding what to eliminate — so you can make time for what needs to get done — requires you to get clear on your goals and priorities.

If you're reading a book about self-discipline, it's because you have projects on your *to-do* list that just don't seem to get done. Maybe you want to start a blog, write a book, launch a business, clean your home or any number of other endeavors.

You might want to start exercising every day or adopt a healthier diet.

Days turn into weeks, into months, into years. You just don't seem to have the time or the focus to take care of business.

Whenever you feel like you don't have enough time or self-discipline to tackle a project, get in the habit of saying, "It's not important to me." It might feel uncomfortable to say at first. After all, you might be talking about a project you're supposed to be passionate about. Let's take a minute to think about that.

What You Do (and Don't)

There are only a few things you **need** to do every day: eat, sleep and use the restroom. After that, everything is optional depending on what is important to you. If you value your teeth, you'll make time to brush and floss every day. If hygiene and appearance matter to you, you'll be sure to shower, shave and comb your hair.

Goals & Priorities

The same idea applies to all the stuff you **don't** do. If you dream about writing a book, but you never make time to write, it's not that important to you. If you want to lose weight, but you refuse to walk around the block or give up those 500-calorie lattés, it's not that important to you. And if you've been talking about a business idea for five years, but you still haven't done any research to see if it's even likely to succeed, it's not that important to you.

"Wait a minute," you might say to yourself. "Those things ARE important to me. I just lack self-discipline. That's why I bought this book."

You have 24 hours in a day. The CEO of a Fortune 500 company and a homeless person begging for change by the freeway also have 24 hours in a day.

Unfortunately, no human being actually gets to be productive for 24 hours every day. Sure, you can do it occasionally with lots of willpower, caffeine or harmful stimulant drugs.

The Self Discipline Solution

How much time does that leave you? Here's a quick breakdown of where most of your time probably goes:

- **Sleeping:** 7 hours
- **Hygiene:** 1 hour
- **Eating:** 30 minutes × 3 meals = 1.5 hours
- **Working:** 8 hours + 1 hour travel = 9 hours

These numbers are different for everyone. Maybe you only sleep five hours per night, take two-minute sailor showers, eat just enough to stay alive, and you live across the street from your workplace.

But for most people, you've got 18 and a half hours of stuff you can't really avoid. That leaves you about five and a half hours to yourself. If you have kids, they're going to account for another large portion of your time. Plus you have to buy groceries, clean the house, mow the lawn, etc.

Goals & Priorities

Two Hours to Dream

Let's just assume that you have one or two hours per day where you can do anything you want. If you spend two hours watching TV, it's already game over. What about that hourlong nap after dinner? Or all that time you spend playing X-Box?

Self-discipline takes just 1-2 hours per day. If your life is particularly busy, it might only take 30 minutes per day. We'll call this your **Dream-Time**.

Your belief that you lack self-discipline stems from the fact that you currently squander that DreamTime on things that don't contribute to your goals. You may enjoy watching TV, but it's at the expense of pursuing your dreams. By eliminating and detoxing from unproductive habits, you make room for that new exercise program, a creative project you keep putting off or that business you want to start.

At the minimum, everyone has to eat, sleep and use the restroom just to stay alive. You can't reduce those activities for very long without serious consequences. The only way to get more time is to cut back on other things. A person who makes a living doing something they love has a nine-hour advantage over someone whose job is unrelated to their goals. Unfortunately, it's unlikely that you're in a position to quit your job to pursue a creative project.

Even if you could quit your job, you are currently incapable of managing one or two hours of DreamTime. Gaining an extra nine hours won't make you more disciplined. If anything, you will become less disciplined because you will have more time to goof off.

A Worthy Sacrifice

No matter what your goal is, there is someone who has done something similar within the same time constraints you have. It's entirely possible to get in shape, write a book or change

Goals & Priorities

the world all while balancing work and family obligations. But your goal has to be important enough that you're willing to sacrifice something else.

It may feel like ripping a bandaid off an old wound. You'll flinch, maybe even scream, when you realize you'll never know how this season of *Game of Thrones* ends. But if your goals are *truly* important to you, you will gladly make the sacrifice.

Don't worry if you decide your new diet, exercise plan or creative project isn't as important as a TV show. It's your DreamTime, and you can spend it any way you choose. At least you're being honest with yourself instead of blaming the problem on a lack of self-discipline.

You don't need anyone else to give you permission. Take control of your DreamTime, and you can accomplish things you never thought possible. Continue treating your precious time as a commodity, and your greatest feat will involve binge-watching the latest TV show.

The Self Discipline Solution

Self-discipline requires sacrifices. If you're not willing to make those sacrifices right now, that's OK. That just means you're being honest with yourself, which is a major step forward. As you continue reading this book — or when you re-read it later — your mindset may be more open to accepting the changes you know in your heart need to be made.

Chapter 4
Avoid Backsliding

"When it is obvious that the goals cannot be reached, don't adjust the goals, adjust the action steps."
— *Confucius*

Most of the heavy lifting is already behind you. You've identified wasteful activities in your day-to-day life and eliminated them. That precious time is now available for more important things.

Now the struggle will be trying to keep it that way. But don't fret. You've got this one.

The way you're going to hold yourself accountable is by setting small goals that will lead you toward your ultimate aim.

If you want to start an exercise program, find a way to add at least 15 minutes of light exercise to your daily DreamTime. You can't go from couch potato to trying to do two hours of Crossfit and expect to stick with it. This is especially true if you don't even enjoy Crossfit, but you chose that because some crazy friend or coworker was raving about its benefits.

The same is true for diets. You can't shift from "I eat what I want when I want" to eliminating carbs, dairy, gluten and anything that casts a shadow. Spend some of your DreamTime each day reading articles and watching videos about nutrition. Plan your meals for the following day. Prep your food so you're not forced to skip breakfast or grab something (unhealthy) on the way to work.

To apply this principle to a creative project, set milestones for yourself so you don't try to do too much too soon. Set a timer, or a word count if you're a writer. Don't listen to reports about how long your idols claim to work on their projects. Just because Stephen King can write all day long, doesn't mean you can (or should) at this point. You're better off using 30 minutes of DreamTime to work on your project *every day* than to work for two hours one day, lose your inspiration and abandon the project for a month.

The Fast Track to Failure

The quickest way to fail — and slip back into your habits of poor self-discipline — is to give yourself a long list of excuses for why it's OK to fail. When you set a big goal with unrealistic expectations for yourself, it often leads to excuses like:

- "This is impossible. I give up."
- "I don't feel good. I'll try again when I'm feeling better."
- "I don't have time for this right now. Life is too hectic."
- "I'm not talented/strong/smart enough to achieve this goal."
- "I'll wait until I feel inspired/motivated. Then I'll succeed."

These excuses, and hundreds of others just like them, mean only one thing: You're trying to lift 1,000 pounds before you can even do a single push-up. The late fitness guru Jack LaLanne once demonstrated on his classic TV show how anyone can lift 1,000 pounds[1].

What was Jack's secret? It wasn't steroids or any other performance enhancing drugs. All he had to do was break the impossible task into smaller pieces, moving a just a few pounds at a time until he'd lifted a total of 1,000 pounds. If you try to lift it all at once, you will fail and revert back to your old bad habits.

Easy Pieces

What if you've broken your goal or project into smaller pieces, but the prospect of success still seems hopeless? There are two ways to move forward.

---

[1] https://youtu.be/cUla2ZB53Yc

Avoid Backsliding

The first solution, as mentioned earlier in this book, is simply to admit that the goal you've set for yourself isn't that important to you. There's no shame in being honest. By admitting this now, you could be saving yourself weeks, months, or even years of your life that would have been spent in pursuit of a dead-end.

Alternatively, you can break your goal into pieces that are so painfully small that it would be impossible *not* to succeed. If you're learning to play a song on a musical instrument, commit to learning the first line of music. If that's too daunting, start with the first measure. And if that's still more than you can handle, start with the first note.

A new exercise plan could start with something as simple as a single push-up or a walk around the block. Failing to perform such a small feat demonstrates a lack of interest, not a lack of self-discipline.

Keep Yourself Accountable

What will happen if you fail to make measurable progress toward your goal?

Will your significant other walk out on you? Will you go bankrupt? Will you die? Hopefully, you answered "No" to each of those questions. But the truth is that no matter what goals you set, you only have a limited time before you shuffle off this mortal coil.

In his acclaimed 2005 commencement speech at Stanford University[2], Apple Computer CEO Steve Jobs told the graduating class that he routinely looked in mirror and asked himself if he would do anything differently if he knew it was his last day to live.

Jobs died of complications related to pancreatic cancer in October 2011. He was 56 years old. During his lifetime, he and his company changed the way millions of people interact

---

[2] https://youtu.be/UF8uR6Z6KLc

Avoid Backsliding

with computers and mobile devices. No matter how you feel about Apple products, their influence is undeniable.

If you knew this was your last day on earth, would you make excuses for why your goals are impossible to achieve? Would you spend your final moments watching television, or spend the remainder of your life feeling tired and out of shape? Probably not.

Would you be satisfied with your obituary if it listed all your accomplishments up to the present? Most people have simple goals, striving to be a devoted spouse, a loving parent and a hard worker. Everyone should hope to be described that way.

But you're different. You're spending precious DreamTime reading a book about self-discipline. You're someone who wants more out of life than to be ordinary. If you're in a relationship, be devoted. If you're a parent, love your children. If you're a working professional, be a hard worker.

The Self Discipline Solution

A life well lived does not include avoiding things that you want to do, while pursuing meaningless activities simply because they are easy or fun.

Memento mori. That's a Latin phrase for: *Remember that you will die.*

Chapter 5
**Become
a Constant Learner**

"Learning never exhausts the mind."
— Leonardo da Vinci

Depending on your goal, it might be virtually impossible to spend all of your DreamTime working on it.

Someone who's accustomed to sitting on the couch can't suddenly spend an hour or two per day exercising. And what about dietary goals? Aside from meal times, it doesn't make much sense to spend two hours thinking about healthy eating.

And you probably won't have one to two hours **every** day to work on your goals. You can't skip out on things like family activities, household chores or taking care of your health.

What if you achieve your small goal for the day and there's still an hour leftover? What if you end up with a few extra hours of DreamTime that you didn't anticipate? Unless you've been practicing the principles outlined in this book for a while, you probably can't trust yourself to work on a creative project for eight hours straight.

Use that time to learn something new instead. Becoming a **Constant Learner** is essential for developing self-discipline. New ideas are essential to building your personal philosophy and finding systems that help you reach peak performance.

The following sections should give you some ideas for how you can spend your time while you're still building up to higher levels of self-discipline.

Become a Constant Learner

Try New Habits

Most people who read books about personal development are new-habit junkies. They're always on the lookout for the latest trends in morning routines, lifehacks, workplace productivity boosters and other tips and tricks from top performers.

Making your life into one big science experiment is a key facet of a self-disciplined lifestyle. The circumstances of life change constantly. There are very few habits and systems that don't break down over time. If you're not constantly exposing yourself to new ideas and challenging your set ways of doing things, you will eventually end up with a toolbox that's poorly equipped for the task at hand.

What are some things that you do every day? Could you do them better? Different? Think about some new habits that would be useful (other than self-discipline) to helping you achieve your goals.

If you're trying to be healthier, try a new kind of floss or toothpaste. Think of some new health foods to put on your grocery list and give them a try. Experiment with different morning routines and bedtime routines.

And if you can't come up with any specifics, read books, blogs or videos to spark some ideas.

A word of caution here: If you get so distracted by researching and trying new habits that you lose track of your goals all together, stop. It's better to spend an hour twiddling your thumbs than actively avoiding important work.

Learn New Skills

Another way to ensure you're constantly gathering new ideas is to learn a skill, or build upon an existing skill.

If your goal is to lose weight by jogging, try out yoga or kettlebells or a spin class (consult your doctor to make sure these are suitable options).

Become a Constant Learner

New skills can be super helpful for creative endeavors. That book you're writing might be even better if you brush up on your grammar, take a graphic design class or study a different style of writing than you're used to.

For every goal, there are countless complementary skills that go along with it. Find one or two and plan to spend some amount of time, however small, working on them. Fresh ideas come from the collision of things you know with things you just learned.

Again, don't get so hung up on these new skills that you completely neglect your major goal. That's only slightly more productive than binge watching Netflix.

Change Your Strategy

When all else fails, do something crazy. That doesn't mean skydiving, buying a one-way ticket to some exotic locale or giving all your money to the next person you see. It definitely doesn't mean doing something immoral or illegal!

This is where some of those wrong suggestions outlined in the Introduction come in handy. Instead of going to bed at 10 o'clock, try going to bed at 8. Try learning how to meditate. Start a diary or journal. Plan a vacation.

Some creative types find inspiration by going for a drive, listening to some good music or going to a public place and watching how people behave. Go for a walk. Try a new kind of restaurant for dinner. You'll be surprised by the things you notice when you deviate from your routine and try something new.

The point is to think outside the box by getting out of **your** box.

A Final Caution

If your initial attempts to become a Constant Learner backfire — meaning you spend more time "learning" than working on your actual

Become a Constant Learner

goals — take a break and revisit these ideas later.

Acquiring new habits, skills and strategies can become a major distraction for some people. Instead of becoming **more** disciplined by focusing energy on things that propel you toward your goals, you may end up trying to justify being **less** disciplined. This is a losing strategy that should be abandoned quickly.

Chapter 6
Make Mistakes Every Day

*"Do not fear mistakes.
You will know failure.
Continue to reach out."*
— *Benjamin Franklin*

Fear of failure is one of the greatest obstacles to success. It can be so overwhelming that you talk yourself out of starting a goal or project in the first place. "What's the point of starting if I'm just going to screw it all up?"

Maybe you've made considerable progress already. Then you mess up your diet by binging on your favorite dessert. Or you start watching a new TV show and completely abandon the novel you were writing.

There will come a day when you can't stop yourself from jumping off the wagon. Days, weeks, months go by and you've done nothing to further your goals. You're not a robot. You're a human being.

In your quest for self-discipline, one thing is certain: You will make mistakes along the way. Even once you have total control over your DreamTime, something is bound to happen that will challenge or completely undermine all that progress.

That's why you have to give yourself permission in advance to make mistakes. Not only that, but you have to get in the habit of making mistakes and being OK with them.

How are you supposed to do that?

Know Thy Self

On some level, you know exactly what you're capable of. You also know your limitations. This knowledge is an essential key to building self-discipline.

Make Mistakes Every Day

Think of something you're not very good at. It could be as simple as balancing your checkbook (or online bank accounts), or as complex as rocket science. Someone who naturally isn't very good at managing their finances is not going to magically get good simply by becoming more "self-disciplined." The same is true for rocket science.

Whenever you set a goal that involves skills that are outside of your natural abilities, you are going to fail. A lot. This doesn't make you a bad person or a failure. It just means you're going against the grain.

A baseball player who hits the ball three out of every 10 tries is considered a high performer. While most endeavors don't permit such a generous definition of success, it's worth thinking about.

Learn From Failure

We've already established that the path on your quest for greatness will be littered with failures. Each time failure rears its ugly head, you have a few choices:

- Quit
- Persist
- Quit and learn from the experience
- Persist and learn from the experience

The first two options involve either giving up or pushing forward without giving much thought to how or why you failed. This is what most people do when faced with adversity. That's why therapists make so much money.

Obviously, options 3 and 4 are much more productive than simply quitting or persisting.

Sometimes it's necessary to quit what you're doing. Either you have physical or mental barriers that make it impossible to continue, or the amount of effort required to persist no longer justifies the benefits. Regardless of the reasons, it's important to understand what barriers forced you to quit so you can avoid similar wasted efforts in the future.

Likewise, the best option may be to push forward to the bitter end. Doing so without reflecting on your failures and assessing whether you can prevent future pitfalls is a grave mistake.

When to Quit

How do you know when to quit and when to persist? It all comes down to your unique goals.

The self-help world is filled with advice about why you should never quit. This is bad advice from people who have likely never attempted anything like what you hope to accomplish.

Maybe you dream of starting your own business. But your initial research about the industry indicates a lack of demand for your product or service, you should absolutely quit. After the demand for Fidget Spinners[3] peaked in May 2017, the market was saturated and the fad had run its course. Scores of entrepreneurs imported the spinning toys from China hoping to cash in on the craze. Within a matter of weeks, sales plummeted, and even major retailers were stuck with tons of unsellable Fidget Spinners.

This is a situation where self-discipline won't help. Quit. Hopefully, the experience will teach you an inexpensive lesson about supply and demand. Seeing a project through to completion even though it's doomed to fail is incredibly foolish.

What if the setback isn't that clear cut? Perhaps you screwed up your diet and exercise plan on day three. That's not a good reason to quit. There's still a high probability that you will succeed. It might require some tweaks to the plan, but success is still within your control.

---

[3] http://bit.ly/2xpnvLo

Chapter 7
Dealing With Burnout

"I am like a man so busy in letting rooms in one end of his house, that he can't stop to put out the fire that is burning the other."
— *Abraham Lincoln*

Assuming you've done everything right up to this point, the question may have crossed your mind about what to do when you're burning the candle at both ends. With great self-discipline comes great responsibility.

Self-discipline is like a string on a violin. Tighten the string too much and it will break. Leave it too loose and it will rattle around like a twig. But if the string is at the proper tension, it can make beautiful music.

Burnout usually manifests in the form of excuses. You suddenly lose the fire in your belly that you had when you began working on this goal or project. Some of the excuses that pop into your head may include:

- "I'm too tired. Maybe I should take a nap instead of working today."
- "Another (*caffeinated drink of choice*) might help me concentrate."
- "I'm going to take a break until I feel inspired."
- "I'm a failure at life."
- "Things are bad and they're never going to get better."

The first thing to do when you first notice signs of burnout is to re-evaluate your priorities. Are you burning out? Or are you simply realizing this goal isn't that important to you? In fact, burnout can be a blessing that prevents you from wasting too much time on a project that isn't worthwhile.

On the other hand, you may have set impossible expectations for yourself.

Make Mistakes Every Day

Climbing Mt. Everest

You can't climb Mt. Everest in an afternoon, no matter how good you are at climbing. First you have to travel from your home to Kathmandu, Nepal or Lhasa, Tibet. This can take between one and three days. Then you have to get to Base Camp, a trek that can take up to two weeks on its own. Once at Base Camp, you have to spend several weeks acclimating your body to the high-altitude atmosphere.

If all goes well, you can expect to reach the summit about two months from your date of departure. Then there's the journey back home, which will take a few more days of travel.

Besides the time commitment, there are also financial considerations. Travel packages to climb Everest cost tens of thousands of dollars.

And even if you have the time, money and skills to make the climb, you could still get injured or killed in the process. At the time of this writing, nearly 300 people on record have died while attempting to climb Everest. Most of those deaths have been attributed to avalanches, falling, collapsing ice, exposure (aka freezing to death), or other health problems related to climate or atmospheric conditions.

Maybe your goal isn't as physically or mentally demanding as summiting Mt. Everest. But it might feel like it, metaphorically speaking.

The best you can hope for is to make **measurable progress in reasonable time**. There's something wrong if it's been six months and you're still hanging out at Base Camp. It either means you're not capable of making the climb or you don't care enough to try.

Even the greatest climbers are no match an avalanche.

Setting Small Goals

When you're feeling burned out, try setting a small goal for yourself. This **micro-goal** can be something so small that it's almost trivial. Write one sentence of your book. Research one aspect of your new business. Do 10 jumping jacks (heck, do one jumping jack if 10 feels like too much).

The important part is to do something productive instead of allowing yourself to do nothing. Burnout is the quickest way to lose momentum. Once the momentum is gone, it can be impossible to start moving again.

Like climbing Mt. Everest, any goal of great magnitude cannot be completed in one fell swoop. Even if you're not ready to summit the mountain, you should at least be developing the necessary skills for the task. A novice climber is almost certain to fail or die if they try to climb a huge mountain before acquiring the skills and physical conditioning for the task.

Take a Break

Sometimes the only way to beat burnout is to take some time off. In fact, burnout often manifests as a complete loss of motivation. That's your body telling you something is wrong.

At times, you will beat yourself up for failing to do the things you wish to do. And that's completely normal unless it lasts for more than a day or two. Beating yourself up can be a powerful motivator. But if it's not pushing you back to the task at hand, it starts to morph into sheer abuse.

When your motivation slips out from under you, everything else of importance follows shortly after. Your mental and physical health, family life, work life and hobbies may suffer. No goal is worth destroying your life over.

When your closest friends or loved ones express concern about your health, assume there is at least a morsel of truth.

Take a week off from your goal. Or a month if necessary. How ever long you need to recharge your batteries and return to the task at hand with joy. Work isn't always easy, but it shouldn't be so hard that it erodes the foundation of your well-being.

Talk About It

Depending on how severe your burnout becomes, people who care about you may start to notice something isn't right. Your instinct may be to assure them that you're "fine" or that you have a lot on your plate right now.

Unless your friends are all psychotherapists, people will usually wait a while to speak up after they notice something isn't right. That means by the time you're hearing the words, "Is everything OK?" they've been watching you for days, weeks or even months.

Even if you're not comfortable talking to the person who asked the question, take this as a sign that you need to talk to someone. Talk to a close friend, relative or significant other.

The longer you bottle things up, the longer it will take to get through the burnout. After talking about the problem, you might decide that you've been approaching your goals with the wrong mindset. What's a "wrong" mindset? It's simply any way of framing a problem that keeps you from making progress.

Maybe you set a goal to lose 100 pounds in six months. After talking it over with a friend, you might realize you've set an unrealistic goal. Or, rather than focusing on losing a specified amount of weight, you might decide you care more about eating healthy.

Consult a professional if you suspect your feelings are more serious than burnout. Anxiety and depression are serious conditions that can't necessarily be treated without professional assistance.

Chapter 8
Be An Inspiration

*"If your actions inspire others
to dream more, learn more, do more
and become more, you are a leader."*
— *John Quincy Adams*

The surest way to succeed at something is to do it for someone other than yourself.

Whether your efforts are motivated by becoming a better provider for your family, or simply showing others that it's possible to make their dreams come true, you are more likely to win.

Goals with selfish motives like making people jealous, showing the world how superior you are, or otherwise harming others, are much more likely to end in anger and frustration.

More importantly, your ambition has to stay true to who you are. Whenever you start to slip away from a place of focus and self-discipline, it's because you don't believe the story you're telling yourself. It's just like when the hero on a popular TV show does something inconsistent with his or her character.

"That character would never do that," you think to yourself.

Unfortunately, few people are capable of quickly reaching such a conclusion about themselves. You decide to start a business selling a popular product that have zero interest in. Or you try to write a bestselling spy thriller even though you love space operas. Or you decide to lose weight by lifting weights even though you hate weightlifting and would rather play basketball with your kids.

When you go against the grain, and do something extraordinary, people will notice. They may mock and ridicule you at first. But one day those critics will disappear, and possibly look to you for advice on how they, too, can do something extraordinary.

Never Imitate

As you consider the lessons from this book and seek to put them to good use, recall the words of Ralph Waldo Emerson's classic 1841 essay *Self Reliance*. The essay immortalized one of Emerson's chief philosophies, namely, that people should avoid conformity and false consistency, instead choosing to follow their own instincts and ideas.

Here is a selection from *Self Reliance*:

> *Insist on yourself; never imitate. Your own gift you can present every moment with the cumulative force of a whole life's cultivation; but of the adopted talent of another, you have only an extemporaneous, half possession. That which each can do best, none but his Maker can teach him. No man yet knows what it is, nor can, till*

that person has exhibited it. Where is the master who could have taught Shakspeare? Where is the master who could have instructed Franklin, or Washington, or Bacon, or Newton? Every great man is a unique. The Scipionism of Scipio is precisely that part he could not borrow. Shakspeare will never be made by the study of Shakspeare. Do that which is assigned you, and you cannot hope too much or dare too much. There is at this moment for you an utterance brave and grand as that of the colossal chisel of Phidias, or trowel of the Egyptians, or the pen of Moses, or Dante, but different from all these. Not possibly will the soul all rich, all eloquent, with thousand-cloven tongue, deign to repeat itself; but if you can hear what these patriarchs say, surely you can reply to them in the same pitch of voice; for the ear and the tongue are two organs of one nature. Abide in the simple and noble regions of thy life,

Be An Inspiration

obey thy heart, and thou shalt reproduce the Foreworld again.

The complete text of Emerson's original essay is available online for free. If you don't have the time or patience to read the entire essay (about 20 pages), consider looking up the Cliffs Notes version.

Maybe Emerson isn't your cup of tea. It doesn't matter where you find inspiration. Just find it. Get fired up and get other people fired up.

Then you will have truly developed self-discipline.

Summary
A Quick Review

This section is designed to help you quickly scan over some of the big ideas described in *The Self Discipline Solution*. It's not meant to be a replacement for reading the whole book. It's simply a compilation of snippets and key concepts.

Sometimes all you need is a little inspiration, not a whole book.

Chapter 1

- A **Goldfish Myth** is a story you've heard so many times that you think it's true, much like the common myth that goldfish have poor memories.

- If you haven't succeeded in becoming more disciplined, it's likely because you have a Goldfish Myth of your own.

- Self-discipline starts with identifying the stories you tell yourself. Which stories are helping you? Which ones are hurting you?

- Ordinary people don't understand why anyone would try to be different. If you're reading a book like this, you probably want an uncommonly fine life. Then you have to be the goldfish that swims the other way.

A Quick Review

Chapter 2

- Whatever your routines are, you have developed a level of discipline to be able to repeat that pattern on a daily basis. Those routines are so ingrained in your life that they require **Extreme Discipline** to continue them.

- It's easier to <u>not</u> do something than it is to <u>do</u> something. Self-discipline starts with **Elimination**, cutting out the routines that prevent you from doing what you want.

- If you give up an Extreme Discipline, your brain will have a hissy fit. Adding new habits or routines too soon will make things worse.

- The **Detox** period should last at least seven days. You'll know you're still detoxing as long as you get a strong urge to continue your old habit.

- It's almost impossible to Detox without doing something to replace the old habit. Just because you've reached the **Replacement** phase, that doesn't mean you're done detoxing.

Chapter 3

- Any time you think you don't have enough time or self-discipline to tackle a project, get in the habit of saying, "It's not important to me."

- There are very few things you **need** to do every day. Everything else is optional depending on what is important to you.

- Everyone has 24 hours in a day. But no human being actually gets to be productive for all of those 24 hours.

- Once you subtract time for eating, sleeping, work and family obligations, you may only have a couple hours leftover. This is

A Quick Review

your **DreamTime**. Master your DreamTime and you master self-discipline.

- Self-discipline requires sacrifices. If you won't make those sacrifices now, that's fine. Just being honest with yourself about that is a major step forward.

Chapter 4

- Hold yourself accountable is by setting small goals that will lead you toward your ultimate aim.

- If you try to do everything all at once, you will fail and revert back to your old bad habits.

- A new exercise plan could start with something as simple as a single push-up or a walk around the block. Failing such a small task shows a lack of interest, not a lack of self-discipline.

- A life well lived does not include avoiding things that you want to do, while pursuing meaningless activities simply because they are easy or fun. **Memento mori**. That's Latin for: *Remember that you will die.*

Chapter 5

- Being a **Constant Learner** is essential for developing self-discipline. New ideas help you build your personal philosophy and find systems to allow you reach peak performance.

- Making your life into one big science experiment is a key facet of a self-disciplined lifestyle.

- For every goal, there are countless complementary skills that go along with it.

- When all else fails, do something crazy.

A Quick Review

Chapter 6

- In your quest for self-discipline, one thing is certain: You will make mistakes along the way.

- Whenever you set a goal that involves skills that are outside of your natural abilities, you are going to fail. A lot.

- Sometimes it's necessary to quit what you're doing. Regardless of the reasons, it's important to understand what went wrong so you can avoid similar wasted efforts in the future.

- The best option may be to push forward to the bitter end. Doing so without reflecting on your failures and assessing whether you can prevent future pitfalls is a grave mistake.

Chapter 7

- You can't climb Mt. Everest in an afternoon, no matter how good you are at climbing.

- The best you can hope for is to make measurable progress in reasonable time.

- When you're feeling burned out, try setting a **micro-goal**, something so small that it's almost trivial. The important part is to do something productive instead of allowing yourself to do nothing.

- Burnout is the quickest way to lose momentum. Once the momentum is gone, it can be impossible to start moving again.

- Sometimes the only way to beat burnout is to take some time off.

- When your closest friends or loved ones express concern about your health, assume there is at least a morsel of truth.

A Quick Review

- People will usually wait a while to speak up after they notice something isn't right. By the time you hear the words, "Is everything OK?" they've been watching you for days, weeks or even months.

Chapter 8

- You're more likely to succeed if your goals benefit other people, not just yourself.

- Goals with selfish motives are much more likely to end in anger and frustration.

- When you go against the grain, and do something extraordinary, people will notice.

- Remember the words of Ralph Waldo Emerson: *Insist on yourself; never imitate.*

About the Author

Mike Eiman is a lifelong resident of Fresno, CA. He graduated from California State University Fresno in 2010 with a bachelor's degree in theatre arts and a minor in mass communications and journalism. He worked as a journalist for seven years, primarily covering local governments, law enforcement and criminal justice.

Today, Mike writes nonfiction, science fiction, as well as articles about the art and business of writing.

For more about Mike, visit www.MikeEiman.com or follow him on social media:

 mikeeimanauthor
 @mikeeiman
 @mikeeiman

www.ingramcontent.com/pod-product-compliance
Lightning Source LLC
Chambersburg PA
CBHW030853180526
45163CB00004B/1559